Andreea T. Niculae

This could be

your story

why no one talks about failure anymore

A true story

2020

Part 1

The beginning of a team

I am writing this story of a major event in our couple lives with the hope that it will inspire you to find the best way to overcome a failure. We keep seeing in mass-media tens, hundreds of examples about achievements, success, people that had a brilliant idea that inevitable led to a huge success and overnight wealth. It might be like this, I don't have a reason to question it, I don't know those people in person, actually, to be honest, I don't know anybody with this kind of evolution.

It's like this outpouring of information regarding the beautiful, rich and extremely happy lives displayed on all the posts on social media that are making you feel "the dumbest from the block", why can't I be like them? At least I thought like that when I was younger until I analysed all the things and realised that, in fact, what people post and how they pose on social media, are just a few seconds from their lives. It's not 24/7 of their time. Nobody is smiling, happy and in vacations 100% of their time.

Let's be real, there are no 100% happy and content people, every day, 24 hours, for an entire lifetime.

We all have ups and downs, we all have less pleasant experiences, a major failure, or two, or three, until you get to a point where you stop comparing yourself to others. You stop comparing your car, your house, your garden, your puppy or your child with what your neighbour from across the street has.

I admit it, now, when I look out the window and see the house and the yard that my neighbour has,

which it's right across the building I live in, I long for only just a small piece with grass where our girl can play all day while I'm relaxing on a comfy deck chair and my husband could make his delicious barbeque. Barbeque with vegetables because that should prevent our neighbours to crave at our grilled minced meat roll.

It's like a dream I wish could come true, a dream that, for the moment, seems so far away.

What made me write these lines? Precisely the failure I had 1 year ago, when I thought that we could make a change in the world. I have in mind now the famous quote: "be the change you want to see in the world."

This failure came exactly when we were the least prepared, (I don't know if there is a proper moment

in life for this kind of experience), when, instead of being happy for delivering our beautiful and loved baby girl into this world and devoting ourselves 100% to her, we were forced to get through hard moments that we don't wish to anybody.

Our love story goes back in 2016 when, after some common acquittances insisted for over 4 months, we got to finally meet in person. From here, everything went smoothly, natural, beautiful and led, after 1 year, to a proposal – that raised to its potential: on top of the Athens heels, among the Acropolis stones.

Yes, I am imagining what you're thinking right now: what a romantic man, that's right, it was an emotional moment, full of romance, hugs and passionate kissing interrupted by the security agent who though that we were to romantics for such a place, full of history and Chinese tourists, in that dry

day of June. The interruption did not upset us, it made us laugh and continue to float on our clear blue clouds.

What happened next? A visit to a jeweller from a bazaar located in the city centre of Athens. You didn't think that the ring was exactly my size, right? I have fingers like a pianist, as my father used to say when I was a little girl. What does a woman do to wear her engagement ring from the first day? She asks every Greek person from the stalls where she could find the nearest jeweller, (our time in Athens was limited, we were in a trip that was going to end in an hour, and we had to get back to the coach).

Yes, I admit it, I am a very stubborn and impatience woman, I could not wait another week, until we would have returned to our country, to resolve this inconvenient. Giving the fact that usually I get what

I want, I found the handy jeweller that "perfectly" re-sized the ring and glued it so good that the poor ring still in the jewellery box, broken.

Days of floating on the clouds went by, we had other trips in wonderful places of the island and, after a week, the moment of returning home arrived.

Oh, I forgot to mention that our closest persons didn't knew the news, so I had to put the ring in the bag until the day we told them. It was a happy atmosphere at home and at work. Inevitable somebody had to ask: "and, have you two set the date yet?". Yes, that's how people are, always one step ahead, you don't let the man enjoy the present and you're already asking about the next step. The wedding day was set in exactly one year after the proposal: it looks like we became in love with the date of 8th of June.

Like you already imagined, the wedding had a Greek theme: from the decorations, chosen colours to my wedding dress, from the candy bar cookies to the cake decorated with olive branches. Olive branches that were found also, of course, in my wedding bouquet. An entire year of preparations, attention to details, searching a wedding band that would mandatory have a repertoire and play Greek music plus the church service performed outside, in the location's garden and planning minute by minute all the itinerary for the day.

You blink twice and the big event is over. You wake up married and with promises, as well, that you will attend other future wedding of your guests in a few years from now. Because, yes, this is the plan for most people: I have to attend this wedding so that they will attend mine when the time comes.

Only a few invited guests came to have a genuine good time, without expecting something else in return. But that's a different story that, maybe, is worth writing about in the future: why are people doing things and always expect something in return? Why they just can't help somebody? Without bragging online and without a reminder that they helped or asking for the given help back.

We planned the honeymoon for a year, as well, another dream came true, (now that I look back; I am really lucky, a lot of dreams became reality, in one way or another, sooner or later), a 14 days itinerary to Morocco. We organised all the details regarding the trip: from the plane tickets, accommodation, car rental and tourist attractions to visit.

I preferred a country so different than all I have visited before because of its uniqueness, because

we don't like luxury or 4 stars hotels, lavender smell and fancy restaurants with waiters wearing white gloves.

In Morocco we found the exact opposite: accommodations in Riads – their traditional houses with a history of over 300 years old, with a main yard, uncovered, with lounges on the rooftop where you can drink a mint tea, (the only one we found there) and you can gaze at the most wonderful sunset. The food was simple, incredibly spiced, semolina pita bread, olives and a lot of hospitality. All is very simple and there is poverty like you would rarely see.

You can find everything here: from policemen with machineguns in the streets or in intersections to hundreds of scooters frenetically running everywhere like scared ants, from pedestrians that don't use the crosswalk and walk everywhere, taking a chance of being hit by cars and scooters that don't respect the traffic rules.

Yes, I am writing from my experience, we slightly hit a woman that jumped in front of our car from nowhere. Fortunately, her and the car's mirror were both in perfect shape.

I have been reading all sorts of stories online before we left: from the Bedouins kidnapping the beautiful European girls and then asking for ransom, to food poisoning from the street food or stone throwing if you walked in a short dress or with your shoulders revealed.

What have we experienced? The best food, so simple that I had the sensation it's made at my momma's house, the most welcoming people, the best and most mint tea, nobody stoled me and nobody wanted to "buy" me from my husband by offering camels in return – we already agreed before we left the country to accept minimum 1000 camels in return. He only has one wife, if he's going to give her away, at least he should receive something valuable in return.

The experience from the desert, walking on the camel's back, sleeping in the tents placed on the sand's dunes, the sunrise and sunset that intensified the red colour of the sand. The surrounding sea of sand and the fear that you could get lost if the guide decided to leave you there, made us fall in love for good with everything that Morocco means.

I felt the fear of getting lost, of getting attacked while driving at night on a road that was parallel to the ocean and it was so dark you couldn't see any other cars. We had no idea how far we were from our next accommodation. Any light coming from sideways was associated with potential thieves that could take those hundreds of euros we had and probably our clothes. Without clothes we could've survived but they should not take our phone as it has GPS and we could get lost for good.

Fortunately, nothing happened and by midnight we reached Essaouira. It also called the wind town, the ocean city, where locals would go to the beach fully dressed. Yes, we were wondering as well how they are tanning? How can they stay fully-clothed on such a wonderful beach at 20 Celsius degrees? You could have seen Europeans from the distance: the only ones in bathing suits.

The second day I understood why they preferred to keep their clothes on and be overdressed, with a blanket over them if it was possible. They prefer salted aerosols instead of a neck pain. Exactly, after a wonderful bikini beach day, on the big, comfortable dock chairs, the next day I woke up with my neck stiffed, I was unable to move my head.

The current, which some say it doesn't exist, the wind or mother nature, got my neck stuck. I can't describe the panic feeling that pain gave me. The honeymoon was already compromised, until the owner of the villa where we stayed, recommended us a special massage in the historical centre – Medina.

A massage was perfect. How can the honeymoon go by without enjoying a massage? The lady over there immediately guessed the cause of my pain and advised me to put some clothes on next time I will walk on the beach or everywhere it's windy – almost everywhere, it's a reason why this town is called "wind town" . Until the evening the pain was almost gone, thanks to her skills. What I haven't told you: in that "stiffed" morning, my husband brought breakfast in bed. On a tray given directly from the restaurant. Apparently, they have a different meaning of "take away": they gave the tray full of food and told him he could pay later, when he will return.

So, my sweet husband walked on the street, from the restaurant to the accommodation with the tray in his hands. The most romantic breakfast I have ever had, even though it had only orange juice, tea, coffee, some Moroccan pita bread, olives, jam and I don't remember having something else. What mattered? The gesture was important and full of love.

Overall, Morocco was a wonderful experience to have at least once in a lifetime, but an experience that doesn't suit just anybody. Here you will feel good and will appreciate places and people for their true worth only if you have an open heart, without expectations. That if you don't mind the garbage smell of the streets, the donkey walking besides you in Medina, the barefoot people, the police with machineguns, the women with barely their eyes at sight or the men that don't turn their heads after the European women and are minding their own mint tea and praying schedule.

If you don't mind trading the perfectly well-made bed from an expensive hotel for a modest bed, with simple bedsheets, not exactly ironed and starched but clean.

It's a country of contrast, where you can find everything. I saw the luxury in the king's palaces but also the filth and extreme poverty from the small towns.

I also met some "neighbourhood boys" that acted like local guides and they usually get you to those labyrinth streets in Medina and, if you don't give them a few euros, they are letting you on your own, which is almost impossible if they lured you on some streets that are not even visible on the map. Every street looks the same.

I could talk about Morocco for hours, that's how much it impacted me and how much I liked it. The most important aspect: in 14 days we haven't heard someone speaking Romanian. We were able to practice some Spanish, a little French, more English or even the body language, the only language you can use to make yourself understood by anybody, anywhere.

Only 2 days after returning home, my husband went to France, for a job training. Just like that, I spent the first 2 weeks of my life as a married woman all alone, like in the good old days.

We left to our honeymoon with the thought of us returning with one more family member, so I gave the new dad the good news over the phone. We celebrated the joy of becoming parents when he returned home.

All was about to change: new teen married life, a new job for him in a completely different domain from his previous job, a baby in my womb – wanted and loved before she choose to come to us and excited to make that change in the world I was talking about in the first lines.

Part 2

From idea to implementation

At the beginning of 2018, before the wedding, we thought of doing the step of having our own business. The ideas were different, at the beginning we thought of having a fitness gym, then a spa with a salted sauna, when, finally, we decided: an artificial salt cave.

We were the happiest people alive. We had a business idea that was completely different and special. We thought that it will work for sure, that people will choose their health over anything else.

So now we begun the Great Adventure, everything was captivating and new.

As we didn't have any savings, we decided to apply for the European funds program, the famous Start Up Nation, started in 2017 and continued in 2018.

In 2017 it was a total chaos, the organizers didn't knew what documents were required, the people winning this program were awake at nights trying to deliver all the requested documents, data and reports, and most of the times the documents were requested without any specific purpose.

But, in 2018, we imagined that everybody knew exactly what to do so, for us, it was the perfect choice.

What's the first step? Finding a consulting firm that could make our project. Not anyone can do such a complex project respecting the legislation, so we choose the safest bet: a consultancy firm.

We found an excellent firm that, of course, didn't do the project for free. Now our adventure begins: a bank loan for the project.

We didn't exactly want to take a loan from the bank but we still believed that it was the winning bet. We start the firm in April, we take a loan, we start learning what it's necessary for this kind of business, we search for suppliers, we organize the entire space – how it should look, from the reception to the salt room.

We anticipated a certain number of visitors based on the existent population from the neighbourhood we lived in, a neighbourhood full of young people that couldn't wait to have a clean and aseptic place to bring their children and to play in.

First mistake: a bank loan when the project was only an idea.

Our excitement was extremely high, the project was kept a secret by the both of us. We want to surprise our friends and family when the project is done.

Why the rush with the bank loan? Because in May the program was opened and the project was supposed to be done, so we had to hurry and get all the things done. Every night, after work, we stayed and collected information, we did calculations, forecasts, we established the entry fee, memberships fees, family packages and so on. We thought about other activities that could've been done in the salt cave as we wanted to be something completely different, new and innovative.

The agent dealing with our project was happy with the provided details and to see us so involved in this. After 2 weeks, the agent quits and another one takes over our project – intern procedure they say. It wasn't a problem, the new girl looked nicer, it was like she understood us better and for sure will do a better project that will win for sure.

After a month all the details were set: the financial part, the list of required equipment and all the necessary paperwork – the project was complete. And now what? We wait for the 2018 methodology (because they wanted to change some details regarding the fonds) to be published, as the one from 2017 was no longer valid. Ok, we wait. May goes by, June and even July were over – we told our agent that we're leaving for our honeymoon and that we'll have our phones near by awaiting the good news.

July, August and September were over, and the program was still on hold. The places we wanted to rent were taken one by one by someone else. The panic settled. And our business? Our days and nights we spent working on this project? Finally, in October, we received the wanted e-mail: the new methodology was published and our project was disqualified from the start. To be able to continue, we had to move the business, the head office and the place of business to a small town, otherwise we can't enter in the competition.

Well, how can we move it? We live in Bucharest, where could we possibly move it? Our agent suggested Dâmboviţa but to go there every day? Absolutely not.

The disappointment was huge, but the work, the gathered information and all the details we knew until that point gave us strength and we didn't gave up that easily.

After we analysed everything, we decided to take a loan from the bank and cover the entire amount. We thought of opening the business ourselves, without the European funds.

The agent from the consultancy firm agrees with us, anyway it would've taken a long time to receive all the money, a lot of paperwork to do, you know how those things with the government work.

The second mistake: the bank loan for the entire amount needed to implement the project

We are no longer analysing things and we're taking the step. We entered from bank to bank until we found one that was on board and gave us the loan. We signed the papers and started to work. Both of us still had jobs and we had a steady income.

My husband has a work from home job and once a month must go on business trips, outside the city. The perfect job that is helping us create our business. We already discussed with the landlord before the loan was approved so we had the space.

It's wasn't a great space giving the location, but it was the only one that we could afford, and it was pretty spacious. We convinced ourselves that the location was important for shops and hair salons, but our business will bring the customers anywhere, even here, on a small street, less circulated. We only found qualities for it.

Third mistake: we underestimated the importance of the location and of the visibility.

At the mid November, we signed the contracts, found the team that handled the artificial salt cave, they brought the salt from Praid at the end of November and in a few days and nights working at it was ready.

On 1st of December, on the room's walls there was the necessary amount of salt, in record time because they had other projects going on but nevertheless pleased with the result and with our design ideas that we requested.

It looked like in the movies, bricks of Himalaya salt with a led band for chromotherapy, which could bring you in a state of complete relaxation from the first minutes. There was also an audio system and a printed wallpaper with a beautiful landscape (2x3m size) that made you feel like you went to the seaside, seeing a stunning beach from Portugal. No other artificial salt cave we found online looked better than ours. We inspired from the ones abroad, we gathered details from more locations, and we got an unique design.

Of course, the rest were different, they went with the cheaper alternative, but we wanted to look professional, to amaze the customer every single time and make walk through our door again.

We even carefully brought some objects for the reception from our honeymoon to bring us luck and to remind us of our implication and about what all this project means to us.

After the salt cave was ready, the time to tell our parents the news has arrived. We wanted them to see at what we have been working on for the last months and to celebrate with us this new chapter of our lives.

The surprise was enormous, they were speechless and couldn't believe that we, alone, did everything that was there, that we thought at everything, from space to the last detail. Indeed, it was extremely hard, hours and days of work. I was convinced that it will be a real success.

It couldn't be otherwise: playgrounds for children with toys to play with in the sand – all the floor was covered in shredded salt, a tiny table and chairs for drawing, folding chairs for adults, audio system, TV with apps and internet, a small library having the National Geographic collection, all the comfort an adult or a child needed to spend 45 healthy and relaxing minutes while playing.

Things were just at the beginning, we had to get the permit to legally operate, to wash and clean the place daily because we were waiting for the Public Health division to inspect it.

After a few days, filed files and made phone calls, we received the much-expected visit. Within days we got the response: the permit was issued. Our dream came true, we could finally bring some value to our community.

In this whole time, until we got the permit, we worked on our website, optimised SEO, as much as we knew – an IT guy was off the table at the moment because it was not in our budget – the Facebook page, the decorations of the showcases – with a much expensive supplier, but the only one available at that time of the year and wasn't that busy printing calendars and notebooks.

In the rush of having it all done, we skipped over the budget, we convinced ourselves that this was really needed and that there is no much time left to wait. The design of an outside showcase has to keep in mind the temperature outside as well, some suppliers are recommending the temperature being higher than 12-15 degrees Celsius or the sticker would fall off. Considering the fact that it was December, the temperature outside was dropping. As we were convinced that the visual part is very important, we ignored our initial budget.

Two weeks it took for the whole place to be prepared and ready until the day we got the permit and we could open for the public. 2 weeks of getting home past midnight because every time something else came up and had to be done, to arrange, to buy and our balance on the current bank account was getting smaller and smaller.

Until the opening day we had the risk and security verification, video surveillance and alarm, and other documents – investments that could have been made in the first 3 month after the opening, but, like responsible and morally correct persons, we choose to do all those things before so that everything could be already done. If someone decided to show up at the front desk for the check up, he or she wouldn't be able to see a string of dust or a missing document.

We literally filled an entire wall with all the documents and announcements that should be displayed in a unit working with the public, beautifully framed, like some paintings waiting for potential buyers.

The baby was growing day by day and the belly was getting bigger but I wasn't worried because she let me help my team mate every day, painting the walls, cleaning, shopping, planning the arrangement of the objects purchased with so much excitement from Morocco – everything so that we can have the perfect Zen, the necessary energy for a big success.

The fourth mistake – an investment way to big regarding the aesthetic part and in check-ups, documents that could have been waiting at least 3 months.

18th of December 2018: the long-awaited day has arrived; we got the phone call that gave us the free pas to open our place. We can make the big announcement, and of course Facebook (which we worked on and got some likes) was our main channel to announce the big opening.

Like any another starting business, we thought that giving a free entry in the first days was the best way to attract the customers – the customer come, see what's all about and they will come back. They have all the reasons to, everything is wonderful, impeccable, the scenery is like a fairy-tale, the toys are coloured and new awaiting to meet their playmates.

The appointments were there – until the opening day we managed to have our own online reservation soft. In exchange of translating it in Romanian they gave us free access for a full year. We were so happy. The customers could make appointments online, in a simple and modern way, we didn't waste any time with phone calls or texts.

The first customers were a few mothers with children, very excited, the children were happy that came to play in the "sand". "It's like at the beach, mommy", one of them yelled.

Our emotions can't be described in words, we gazed into each other's eyes, proud of the result. The people loved it, they complimented us and said that they can't wait to return. What can be more beautiful than seeing the happiness in the eyes of the children and the parents being so relaxed.

Now they have a place, close to their homes, where they can breathe a fresh air, especially with all the polluted air and the dust surrounding us every day. The first 3 days of free entry were beyond any expectation. The customer came in, did their 45 minutes session of halotherapy and left happy, with the promise of their return.

We were the happiest tired people on the face of the earth. Our effort was rewarded. The people will come back, they said that and even left wonderful reviews on Facebook.

I wonder when we will have to hire someone to stay at the front desk and help us with all these excited customers? The plan was that in the next 3 months to hire someone because the baby was due April and I wouldn't be able to handle it.

According to our initial calculations, and with the customers confirmations, the ones that came in the first 3 days after the opening day, in 3 months for sure we'll be able to hire someone.

We chose to keep the place open from Monday to Saturday so that on Sunday we could rest. Giving the fact that we were tired and exhausted, we weren't able to anticipate things. We needed at least one free day a week. We even shared the workday in shifts: in the first part of the day I was staying at the front desk so my husband could work from home for his job without neglecting his commitments there. Giving the advanced pregnancy, I was able to get a maternity leave and my job was no longer a concern.

The "free entry" days went by and now the customers must pay a modest fee to have access in the salt cave. The prices were the same as our competitors, decent prices I would say, below of how much a pack of cigarettes would cost. Of course, children would get a 50% off discount.

We wouldn't want to have some prices below what's on the market and be accused of dumping. We choose to play fair, to not get mad at anybody, especially that this town is so populated and there are clients for everyone.

The hours were passing and our soft would not register any appointments. We were at the beginning, we had to be patient until our neighbours find out. In 2-3 days, the appointments begun to appear. People were still content with our services, with the fresh air they were breathing, with how well them and their children felt after the halotherapy sessions.

December was quickly over, with the receipts that satisfied us, under what we had predicted, though, but offering a good start, nevertheless.

The emotions were as big as before. In the hours we had lots of customers we were excited, and we had confidence boosts, believing that it's impossible to happen something bad now.

We made plans to change the front desk design to be able to receive more customers at once.

Some changes were made within the few days. This is what we loved at being our own bosses: we didn't have to ask for permission and to explain why we want to move things around.

We were taking the decisions and put them in practice in the shortest time possible, depending on the requests.

Within the first days we spoke to the kindergartens in our neighbourhood to offer the possibility to do some of their optional classes in our salt cave but without a positive feedback from their side.

We wanted to have different services so we searched and found a yoga instructor for adults and one for kids.

From the 3rd of January, we offered the possibility to work out in the salt cave, with guided breathing in such a healthy environment that you couldn't refuse. One of the yoga instructors just got back from India where she graduated a course in breathing methods.

These activities costed money: equipment and the trainers salary. The bank account balance was dropping day by day.

January had a slow start with only a few customers in days. We found some reasons for that: people celebrated the winter holidays, their wallets are tight because they went to holiday, they're tired, it's pretty cold outside and the list of reasons can go on.

After a week, the things begun to change. A few customers appeared every day but we're taking it step by step. We know we must have patience.

In this whole time we kept investing in ads: Facebook, Google Ads, flyers at the subway station or on the street, flyers glued to the poles with the salt cave's details on them all over the neighbourhood, newsletters, personalized balloons, website SEO, promotions and offers, free entry days for children, discount days for couples, memberships, vouchers, discounts for registering on known websites, contracts with firms that provided memberships for their employees to spend their free time.

We had the surprise to welcome customers from other neighbourhoods that are far away from us telling that they saw the "Facebook Ad". A confirmation that social media advertising works and the money are worth investing in it. We ended January optimistic, with the hope that from now on the number of our customers will constantly rise and we could reach the wanted number.

We were aware that the number of customers, especially children, was depending on their school holiday but at least we paid our rent for the upcoming month, it was a really good start.

A good friend from our neighbourhood helped us with the dance lessons in the salt cave, a very special and unique experience that couldn't, unfortunately, get more than 3-4 persons in class. It was good as it was, giving the fact that our friend didn't want something in return and just wanted to help us. We're still thanking him. He was one of the few persons that actually did something to help us.

February started with a letter from a law firm informing us that we have to close our business within the next 24 hours.

As we were reading, our mind was unable to process the information. We were accused of using the name of a fitness club to get new customers.

A part of our name was like sounded like theirs, a letter was different – we chose the name by doing an anagram from our and our parents initials, we thought it was funny and it also sounded very good.

Our logo was made by an Indian freelancer and, surprisingly, it was very much alike with the one the fitness club had.

The fifth mistake: trusting the graphic designer. We should have checked the logo on Google to see if there are any similarities to other logos.

We discussed with a lawyer that advised us to keep it simple, not complicate things, that their brand is registered and, even if the word differs by a letter, they will win the case and we can risk even a fine in addition to closing the business.

The sixth mistake: We should have verified at OSIM the name of our firm to see if the name is or isn't a registered brand.

From Friday to Monday we made up a new name for our brand, contacted another freelancer for a new logo (this time we verified it on Google, we learn from our mistakes), we ordered the new stickers, new front desk logo to hang on the wall, we bought a new website domain, we changed the Facebook name, the graphic for the new flyers which we later ordered. Did we get some sleep in those days? I can remember for sure.

But what I do know is that, the moment I laid in bed, I wonder if my beloved baby kicked me with his tiny feet in the last hours or I was just so stressed that I didn't even feel it or noticed.

In the following days we explained the customer why, after over a month from opening, we suddenly had to change our name.

Some said that the old name was better, that the new one doesn't have the same impact – exactly what we needed, another punch in the face added to the others and to those days and nights we continuously worked.

We reached to a point where we would encourage ourselves: a name is subjective, each person perceives it differently, anyway it's already water under the bridge, the important thing is to move forward and to be optimistic, now that a growth period is following.

The seventh mistake: not making a budget special for unpredictable expenses which have definitively destabilized the bank account balance.

We continued to spend our money of advertising: Facebook, Google Ads, flyer and banners. The result? We had no new customers. We already had some regular customers, some grandfathers and grandmothers brining their grandsons over in the children's holiday or days off from the kindergarten.

A hand of people knew how to appreciate this type of business and put their health and their children's health first and found a warm, special, close to their homes place where they could simply relax and spend a quality time with their loved ones.

February was over and the results were concerning: the receipts were lower than the previous month. Even though, apparently the number of customers was bigger, so were the expenses. Our bank account balance was therefore still negative.

Our motivation to keep going were the wonderful children that begged their parents to bring them here, over and over again, to the "salt brine", to play in the shredded salt and make yoga with a story every Saturday morning.

It was such an overwhelming feeling when you saw that you can make some children happy. In their innocence, they really appreciated our work more than their parents and adults did.

The neighbourhood we lived in had no green spaces, no parks nearby. The parents were walking their children among parked cars, in parking lots breathing the dust and polluted air left behind by cars.

This exactly why I thought about a totally safe, clean and aseptic playground – bacteria can't grow because of the salty environment, this playground is one of the healthiest and cleanest places compared to the ones you can find in malls or parks.

We put on a wall a huger banner with the benefits of the salt therapy, explained for everybody. We also posted on Facebook and on the website. But, no matter of what approached we chose, we were unable to get the necessary daily customers we needed.

We read comments and discussions on different groups where people, that had no idea where the salt cave was, told how bad for a child is such a playground. The people from those group were enjoying "being seen" and could influenced others.

And all of that for what? Because we didn't want to pay our customers to give comments and posts in our favour. Usually our posts on those groups were erased.

In the first week of March, the baby decided to joined us with a month sooner. As there was no one who could've managed the appointments and the advertising, we decided to close the salt cave for a week. At least until we can have a chance to get used to this new family, especially since the baby was premature and needed more attention.

After a week, we decided to open only when we had appointments, as we didn't want to lose time staying at the front desk waiting for customer that wouldn't show up.

We continued our work from home with newsletters, flyers at the subway station, on the streets, on the cars, with paid ads on Facebooks, banners on the front door, in the neighbourhood and a neon sign.

We had a lot of different activities:

- Yoga classes
- Creation workshops for children
- Yoga for kids
- Physiotherapy workshops
- Support groups for moms suffering from post-partum depression with an experienced psychologist
- First aid classes teched by the ambulance staff
- Speech therapy courses for children with problems.

For all these workshops, we searched for qualified staff from the neighbourhood #WeSupportCommunityGrowth, we set up modest prices that could cover all the expenses we had with the trainers.

None of the workshops happened because there were only 2 persons that signed in, even though we and our trainers struggled with the advertisement.

The eighth mistake: the lack of a feasibility study to see what impact such a business would have in the chosen area.

What we have been able to observe so far? There are few people that realize the fact that they need other types of workshops and experiences, who understand how important it is to accumulate new knowledge. And most importantly, just few understand that the persons holding these workshops has the right to be rewarded for his/hers work and time and it cannot always be free.

We only want what's free, it doesn't matter if we really need it, but what relevance does it have? I remember that some friends, who recently opened a coffee shop here, in the neighbourhood, in the first 5 months since they opened it, they haven't seen any significant increase in the number of customers, no matter how much advertising or activities they have brought to their coffee shop.

A few days ago they told me they had a promotion called "Free Coffee To Go on Monday" and they have customers but, as you probably already guessed, only on Mondays and some of them are even coming more than once, saying that "if it's for free, why not?".

Probably this type of behaviour is linked to the education received in childhood. Or maybe the poverty, selfishness – why should I make a person rich, perhaps it's just a poor set of priorities or values in life.

Going back to our salt cave, the things keep getting harder and harder. My husband can no longer work from home as his bosses told him to go to one of the Hubs. In the first days, I took the baby with me when we had appointments. The same regular customers that really appreciate the relaxation coming with their children. The kids are happily playing, without any worries and they return home with their clothes white, with salt in their hair and mouth but amused about what they did.

They are no longer just simple customers; they are already from our acquittances circle. They share their opinions about the business, about how they think the things are going. They tell us to be patient as they're recommending us as well, trying to convince their family and friends of the benefits this place has.

Slowly, even the regular customer are coming from time to time. Neither myself, nor my husband, could deal with the advertisement anymore, there was no time left between the main job and the baby. The bank account balance dropped so low that we could barely afford to pay rent and utilities.

There were required a lot of money for the advertisement. Facebook changes it's algorithms every day, the last month's targeting doesn't get new customers this month. Our posts stopped reaching the relevant people. Our budget was limited so we couldn't hire some experienced publicity agency that could handle the advertisement on our behalf. We should've had thousands of euros to invest for a really good, professional advertising, on a long term that could also bring us results in the meantime. Time that we no longer had as the budget was getting smaller and smaller.

Days of real struggle and stress followed, from our personal income we couldn't pay the bank loan, therefore we went to the bank, explained the situation we got a 10 year debt repayment re-schedule, 10 years in which we' ll have to pay for a dream that turned into a failure.

10 years, month by month we have to give most of our income to the bank, money wasted on design and rent.

If in April we had a few customers, in May nobody showed up. We decided that it's the moment to quit, no matter how much it hurt and no matter how much we kept on postponing this discussion.

We initially tried to sell it, maybe if someone comes with capital to invest in advertisement, they could make it work. Our work, effort and money invested cannot be thrown away like that.

We place ads on all profile sites, we get in touch with different people with money who could make such investments. Everybody said the same thing: very nicely arranged, I've never seen anything like it, but it's not the kind of business for me. The planets didn't line up for us, we didn't find anyone interested. The money left in our account was enough for us to pay exactly only one moth of rent: May.

We took the final decision: to close it down permanently, to sell what can be sold and move on. The problem was that the room was lined with salt, there were tons of salt, lumps and shredded, we could not sell it, no one would have bought it. The builders don't want to relocate it. It costs more to demolish, transport and install it in another location.

It's the last weekend from May and we had to clear out the space. If we put the inventory items up for sale on the internet and they will be sold, the salt had to be stored somewhere. I chose, as a lifesaving solution, my grandparents' house at country side. The transport there implied another high cost that we hadn't thought of for a second 6 months ago.

Saturday night the van came, took the salt and drove to my grandparents. The lovely people woke up with half a yard full of salt, they did not understand much of all our decisions, but they supported us unconditionally and didn't ask questions that would've made us feel worse than we already had.

The family helped us to demolish, to remove the salt from the walls, the ceiling and the floor and to storage the inventory items. We had them beside us at the opening: with champagne and cakes, and at the closing: with dust and sadness.

On the 1st of June we handed over the space. Of course, we lost the rental guarantee, the space didn't look the same anymore, it needed modifications, repairs, all the salt on the walls and ceiling left traces. Although we tried to clean and repair, we needed craftsmen to do this work plus a lot of time that we no longer had.

6 months of work, sleepless hours, plans, emotions and advertisement ideas, all died in a few hours.

The lack of an adequate budget for advertisement and an amount of money for backup, to support the periods without receipts, have had their word. In our enthusiasm we did not take into consideration the power of high-level advertising, we were subjective and dreamy, believing that we can attract customers through simple sponsored posts with small amounts of money invested and a few flyers offered on the streets.

I didn't have the strength to go when our families came to help us demolish. I could not see how a dream for a better life, a desire to help the community in which we live, could not be fulfilled.

When I finally had the courage to go, it wasn't much left, our space was no longer ours and our decor items were in bags. I don't think I've ever felt such a disappointment before. 6 months ago, I dreamed with my eyes open about how our child will play with the clients children, how she will take her first steps through the reception and put her tiny hands on the shredded salt on the floor. None of this was possible anymore.

The last mistake: the impatience to sell the inventory items as soon as possible, at half of the price we paid, just to get rid of them and to free up the space in which we had stored them.

The salt finally went, after a few months, to an animal farm with no charges and no profit.

As I write these lines, it is exactly one year has passed since we had to shut down our business, a year in which we got to bed every day and woke up with the image we had in the salt cave, a printed landscape on a 2 x 3 m, of beautiful beach in Portugal. We couldn't sell it so we put it in our bedroom.

My husband said that it's an everyday reminder of his failure, but for me, it's a reminder of the dream we had together, of doing something for our child and for those in the community where we live. What's left to do? The dreaming woman remains

 dreamy until the last day of her life. There, somewhere in the depths of my soul, I think the day will come when my way of thinking and acting will make a difference in this world which is agitated, selfish, in a constant motion, and always rushing... to nowhere.

The body of a pregnant woman, who is later also breastfeeding, produces oxytocin, a hormone that makes the pain during pregnancy and childbirth easier to feel then, after birth you have the strength to be able to take care of the baby, even with very few hours of sleep per night. But for me, it also had the effect of making me detach myself more from the problems, from the disappointment, from not panicking due to such a failure and a loan that takes away most of our family income.

I often think that maybe this experience came at the right time, when I had the mental and emotional strength to assimilate all these changes.

But not everything was all black. In those months we knew wonderful people from whom we had something to learn. We were able to contribute to the visible improvement of the health of a 10 years old child who, after years of medication, could not get rid of a cough that bothered him most of the time. He was among our first customers, which remained in our hearts and in those moments offered us the confirmation that we made the best decision to offer this place to people.

Parents who came to the salt cave constantly told us how happy their children were and how good they slept and ate after the salt therapy sessions. How they want to come by themselves to the playground with the sand and "saline aerosol" as often as possible - as they called the place.

We still meet people on the street who tell us "I have such a bad cough, how good would've been your salt cave now". We are somehow happy to see that we were appreciated by a few people who understood our purpose there. But with a handful of people you can't run a business, you can't pay rents and utilities, and moreover, you can't pay the loan at the bank.

Unfortunately, very few people understood the usefulness of such a business and our budget, far too small, could not sustain the months, perhaps the years it would have taken to change people's thinking and attract new customers constantly.

The forecasted figures were not reached in any month of operation. We needed 4 -5 customers per hour, 8 hours a day, from Monday to Saturday, with a population of over 50,000 people and no green space nearby. How to anticipate that those few customers will not come, that they will prefer the "dust alternative", that they will take their children to some parking lot of a supermarket?

In the days when we had the promotions with free entry for children, there were parents who asked us if they could leave the children of 2-3 years alone in the salt cave, unattended, just so they would not pay the entrance. Our rules were clear from the day one, no child will be left unattended so we could to avoid various unpleasant situations with other customers or any injuries.

What did I notice from this experience? Most people want to receive things for free, anything, anywhere, it doesn't matter if they need it or not. They promise they'll come back, but they don't.

Another very important aspect that I noticed, and that hurt a lot more: people you consider friends, close, even relatives, can change their attitude in a very short time.

Envy is so present in many of us. Why should the other get rich? Why wont the neighbour's goat die too? Why didn't I had this idea first? Relatives that you considered part of a close family, for which you have been putting your partner and child in second place, did not even have the curiosity to pay a visit, to see what you have been working on all this time, in what you have been investing all resources in.

On such occasions, you see who is truly your friend, who is truly supportive and happy of your success, or who's beside you in case you encounter problems. For us, this list is very short: we have our family and some very close friends. And the list ends here. If you compare this list with the lists of "friends" on Facebook or from WhatsApp groups, is representing how much: 1%?

Because the reality is other, very different from the hearts and pictures with food and holidays on social networks.

Because now we don't have time to think about the others, to offer unconditional help, to be happy for the success of others, to come up with an idea, maybe it will be useful.

Disappointment comes from many directions, but it is only up to us how we chose to greet it.

I chose to keep the beautiful memories, the laughter of the children when they saw how they could pick up the salt dust, the fascination in their eyes when I showed them the videos from the salt cave and saw what the aerosols they inhaled look like. The colourful drawings during the halotherapy sessions that they gave us as a gift to put on the panel specially arranged for them.

All the things I have learned from accounting, marketing, public relations, putting ideas into practice, legislation, identifying opportunities, contacting strangers to give them the opportunity to associate, all these things will for sure help me in the future.

If you are wondering if I would do this project again: most likely yes. I am convinced that I could have done more. I consider that I have the obligation to at least try to fulfil it.

If I only think about it and wait for the luck to find me, it's a bit difficult to get something. I prefer to regret something I did, even if it did not bring the expected result, then to regret something that remains just an idea and to ask myself all my life "what it would have been like to…".

But yes, I would do things differently, I would not repeat the mistakes we made, I would not make unnecessary investments, I would choose the most suitable location, I would do a market study to find out the preferences of the inhabitants of that area before taking any decision, and most certainly I would not do business in this neighbourhood but I would choose a different one.

Instead, I would no longer ask the bank for a loan covering the entire amount, and I would expect to have some saved money that would give us a certain degree of stability.

But as mistakes are paid for, you will first have to pay the bank loan for this closed business before demonstrating your true potential.

This time wasn't lost and for sure it wasn't an experience we would want erased from our memory.

Life sucks... You fall, you get up, you learn from it and you move on.

Don't give up on your dreams - one day, sooner or later, they will come true!